BOOK ANALYSIS

Written by Éléonore Quinaux
Translated by Jessica Foster

AF131352

Ulysses

BY JAMES JOYCE

JAMES JOYCE

IRISH POET AND NOVELIST

- **Born in Dublin (Ireland) in 1882**
- **Died in Zurich (Switzerland) in 1941**
- **Notable works:**
  - *Chamber Music* (1907), collection of poems
  - *A Portrait of the Artist as a Young Man* (1916), novel
  - *Finnegans Wake* (1939), novel

James Joyce came from a large family and had a Jesuit education before rejecting Catholicism at the age of 16. Later, he developed a similar way of thinking to that of Thomas Aquinas (Italian priest, 1225-1274). He spent the majority of his life in exile in order to distance himself from Ireland, whose immobility and religious divisions he detested, and with which he never managed to identify.

Initially roaming between Paris and Dublin, it was in Switzerland – where he taught at the Berlitz School – and in Italy where Joyce found refuge with Nora Barnacle (1884-1951), his partner. From 1906, he was afflicted with an eye condition which caused him to go gradually blind.

Although he was admired by many great figures of international literature, Joyce only got by on the donations of his rare admirers. He visited Marcel Proust (French writer, 1871-1922) in Paris in the 1920s and befriended Samuel Beckett (Irish writer, 1906-1989). Knowing he was nearing the end of his life, he returned to Zurich in 1940 where he died some time later. A real literary oddity, he was misunderstood and not widely read in his time.

ULYSSES

A HUMBLE EPIC

- **Genre:** multi-genre novel
- **Reference edition:** Joyce, J. (2000) *Ulysses*. London: Penguin.
- **First edition:** 1922
- **Themes:** Dublin, society, romantic relationships, sexuality, roaming, identity, myths.

Ulysses appeared as a series in the American magazine *The Little Review* between 1918 and 1920, then as a book in 1922.The title immediately informs the author of the link between this novel and the *Odyssey*, the famous epic by the Greek poet Homer (8th century BC). The story unfolds over a day in Dublin and is centred around two characters: Stephen Dedalus, the author's alter ego, embodying a new Telemachus; and Leopold Bloom, an advertising agent, the new Ulysses whose quest consists of winning back the love of his unfaithful wife, Molly.

The story, considered obscene by Joyce's contemporaries, was banned in the United States until 1931, although Hemingway (American writer, 1899-1961) circulated several volumes. Its rich narrative now means that we consider it as a major 20th century work.

SUMMARY

In *Ulysses*, the events take place from 8am until around 3am the following day. Although this summary keeps the temporality set out by the story, it does, however, compare the main actions of Leopold Bloom and Stephen Dedalus, which are recounted in different parts of the novel. The unexpected developments of the story and its three-part structure – 'The Telemachiad', 'The Odyssey' and 'The Nostos' – directly recall Homer's *Odyssey* as well as the characters of Telemachus and Odysseus. In order to understand the symbolic significance present here, the reader will find, for each protagonist who represents the alter ego of a key character in the Greek work, their name in brackets.

GOOD TO KNOW

The *Odyssey*, written after the *Iliad*, is an ancient epic attributed to the Greek poet Homer and dating back to the 8th century BC. Its main protagonist is Odysseus (Ulysses in Latin), King of Ithaca. After fighting in the Trojan War, he wants to return home to join his wife Penelope and his son Telemachus.

However, his journey back to those lands will last ten years, a journey during which he will be diverted from island to island and will meet mythological figures that are still well-known today. While he roams, Telemachus does everything he can to find his father and to thwart the crowd of suitors who wish to marry his mother just to steal the throne. To do this, he will seek advice from

Nestor – one of the very few companions of Odysseus who has returned home without trouble – and from Menelaus, the King of Sparta.

Odysseus takes so many years to get home because he is subject to the vengeance of the god Poseidon after injuring his son Polyphemus. In particular, he is held prisoner of love by the sea nymph Calypso for seven years. When she receives the order from the gods to release Ulysses, she obeys. Poseidon then creates a storm which causes the hero to wash up on the coast of Scheria. There he meets Nausicaa, daughter of the King Alcinous. Odysseus tells her about his run of bad luck: the help that he had received in vain from Aeolus, his encounter with the sorceress Circe who changed his companions into pigs, the Sirens' evil song and Calypso.

The Phaeacians are moved and agree to help Odysseus by taking him back to Ithaca. When he hears about the scheming of Penelope's suitors, Odysseus must find a strategy: he disguises himself as a beggar with Athena's help and seeks help from his faithful swineherd, Eumaeus. During a final test that will decide who Penelope's new husband will be, Odysseus manages to draw his legendary bow and kills Antinous, the leader of the suitors. He thus reveals his true identity.

A BUDDING QUEST

In the bay of Dublin, Stephen Dedalus (Telemachus) and Buck Mulligan (Antinous) live in the Martello tower of

Sandycove. Their morning discussions revolve around two matters:

- Buck, although a freethinker, reproaches Stephen for not going to his dying mother's bedside to pray;
- Stephen complains about Haines (Eurymachus), an Englishman who lives in the neighbouring room and screams all night.

After breakfast, marked by a milkman stopping by, each of them states their activities: Buck wants to go for a swim in the sea, Stephen has to go to the school where he teaches, while Haines opts to go to the national library.

At that very moment, Leopold Bloom (Odysseus/Ulysses) decides to make breakfast for himself and his wife Molly (Penelope) but, overcome by a sudden craving for kidneys, he goes to the butcher to buy some. When he returns, he finds two letters in the mailbox, one from his daughter and the other from a man whom he knows to be his wife's lover, Blazes Boylan. His wife is indeed continually absent and is unfaithful to him. As for Bloom, he is often lonely and constantly plagued by sexual desires that go unsatisfied. After discussing the meaning of 'metempsychosis' (reincarnation of the soul after death) with his wife, he sets off on a walk through Dublin, to get to his neighbour's funeral.

DUBLIN THE LABYRINTH

When Stephen finishes his history lesson, the head teacher, Mr Deasy (Nestor), an old anti-Semite, calls him into his office so that he can pay him. Knowing that the young teacher is also a writer and therefore in touch with editors, Deasy takes advantage of this by demanding that he get his article on foot-and-mouth disease published.

At the same time (10am), Bloom goes to the post office to collect a letter from Martha, with whom he has a romantic connection, although he has never met her, and she only knows him under the pseudonym 'Henry Flower'. The message that he receives excites him and he continues his journey with a head full of lustful thoughts. He catches the end of a Mass, which sends him to sleep as usual, then goes to the pharmacy, where a misunderstanding occurs: Bloom meets Bantam Lyons who wants to borrow his newspaper to read the horse-racing bets. The two men misunderstand each other: Bloom is talking about throwing away his newspaper, while Lyons thinks he is getting a tip for betting (one of the horses is called Throwaway). Before going to the funeral, Leopold goes to some public toilets and masturbates, to relieve all the sexual tension that he has endured during his journey.

At 11am, on Sandymount beach, Stephen is depressed and thinks about his successive failures: abandoning his medicine degree in Paris, failing as a writer and being forced to become a teacher. He feels down about his luck, as he thinks that intellectual freedom goes hand in hand with loneliness. As for Bloom, it is now time for him to go to Glasnevin cemetery. The group that gathers there reminds him of his own sorrows: the death of his son, Rudy, and his father's suicide. Among those present is a stranger wearing a waterproof macintosh, which deeply intrigues him.

At midday the paths of the two main protagonists cross: they go to the printing room of a local newspaper, the *Freeman's Journal*. Bloom wants to renew an advertisement for one of his clients. The director, Myles Crawford (Aeolus), receives it. Stephen has come to publish Mr Deasy's article. Although they are briefly together in the same room, the two men do not directly converse.

Bloom is hungry after this, and after bumping into several acquaintances, decides to go to Burton to eat. But once he is there, the overcrowding, stenches and mouths full of food repulse him. He changes his mind and goes to Davy Burne's. But the shape of the bar reminds him of a female body and suddenly he starts to wonder if statues have anuses. To find the answer, he goes to the national library where Stephen is giving a conference on William Shakespeare (English writer, 1564-1616) and the father figure in *Hamlet* (1601).

Everyone leaves the library. After meeting many of the characters described in 19 sketches (which show that the events of daily life have no real impact on the plot), Bloom has lunch at around 4pm at the Ormond hotel with Stephen Dedalus' uncle, Richie Goulding (Menelaus). The waitresses (the Sirens) make fun of him and prefer to flirt with Boylan, who leaves soon after to meet Molly. While some people, such as Simon Dedalus, Stephen's father, sit around the piano and sing, Bloom writes a letter to Martha.

FOG, HALLUCINATIONS AND REBIRTH

At 5pm, Leopold Bloom is meant to meet a friend, Martin Cunningham, at Barney Kiernan's tavern. When he enters the pub, several people are having a discussion, including 'The Citizen' (Polyphemus). Bloom is then invited to this man's table, whose personality is radically different from his own. He is an aggressive nationalist, while the main character embodies gentleness and tolerance themselves. Getting wind of the advice he gave to Lyons for betting, everyone present thinks that Leopold has won a large sum of money from the horse racing. However, he doesn't buy his round, which incites their hatred. Noticing their anger, Bloom decides to leave the place with Cunningham once he has arrived, with anti-Semitic insults shouted after him.

On the beach, Gerty MacDowell (Nausicaa) – The Citizen's niece - is dreaming of what her life could have been like. Suddenly, she realises she is being watched by an old man in dark clothing; it is in fact Leopold. When a firework is set off, thus distracting everyone on the beach, the young girl lifts her skirt so that Bloom can enjoy what is underneath. He is aroused and masturbates in front of her. Thinking of female desire, then of menstruation, he decides to go to the maternity hospital to see Mrs Purefoy, who is soon to give birth. There is quite a crowd present – including Stephen – who celebrate as the mother-to-be cries.

At midnight, in Mabbot Street, Bloom – who has been following Stephen and his friend Lynch, who are both drunk – wanders into the red light district. Suddenly, he starts having hallucinations which remind him of all his faults, his inappropriate desires or his guilt with regard to his loved ones. Passing near Bella Cohen's (Circe) brothel, he hears Stephen playing the piano. The tune lifts Bloom from his drowsiness and he goes inside to join the two friends. But his hallucinations begin again after he is propositioned by the prostitute Zoe Higgins: he imagines himself as a king-chairman, then as an emperor-president who would reform the entire country and be considered a Messiah. The prostitute awakens him from his nightmare and explains the hidden meaning of the lines on his hand, while Stephen lectures on the apocalypse. Strange visions overpower the two men: Bloom sees his grandfather wearing a macintosh and Stephen sees his dead mother who begs him to repent. Yelling *'Non serviam'* ('I will not serve', one of Satan's sayings), the professor sets about breaking everything in the establishment before fleeing. Bloom pays for the damages. Stephen is violently attacked by British soldiers and collapses in the middle of the street, before Bloom takes responsibility for him. The latter then has a final vision of his dead son.

Bloom takes his friend to the cabman's shelter, an establishment owned by Skin-the-Goat Fitzharris (Eumaeus), whom we believe to be a former terrorist. After several discussions about the existence of God, he shows Stephen a photo of his wife and invites him for a cup of cocoa at his house. Thus, at 2am, they drink their hot chocolate and discuss various subjects, such as Ireland, Israel or their mutual friends. Leopold offers to house him for the night, but Stephen refuses. They end their conversation in the garden, looking at the illuminated window of Molly's bedroom, then Bloom accompanies Stephen to the street and the two friends finally part.

Now alone, Bloom ponders Molly's infidelity, but remains in denial by not holding her accountable, despite the fact that he knows she is unfaithful. He goes up to bed, lying next to his wife, who asks him about his day. He is tired and eventually falls asleep. Molly, still very much awake, gets lost in her thoughts and begins a highly obscene monologue in which she seems to present herself as fertile ground. She laughs at men, at their perverse desires and at her lovers. She lets out a wave of urine into her chamberpot, representing her flow of words, and realises that she is menstruating: a new cycle begins. She thinks once more about Bloom's marriage proposal and the 'yes' she gave him: a 'yes' to life, to the entire universe that she must surrender to.

CHARACTER STUDY

In *Ulysses*, we find many characters scattered along the streets of Dublin who, above all, enable Leopold and Stephen to evolve. We have therefore chosen to focus on the main contributors to this evolution. A note on the man in the macintosh is also included, as this character raises many questions in criticism or commentaries on Joyce's work. We therefore deemed it important to pay attention to his characteristics.

STEPHEN DEDALUS (TELEMACHUS)

Stephen Dedalus appears to be the spitting image of the author, whose full description is given in a previous novel by James Joyce, *A Portrait of the Artist as a Young Man*. After a Jesuit education, the protagonist starts to increasingly reject religion, changing status from Roman Catholic to agnostic. While he was supposed to continue studying medicine in Paris, we learn at the beginning of *Ulysses* that he returned to Dublin on account of his dying mother. His opposition to Catholicism leads him to refuse to say any prayers at her bedside. This event later haunts him, as maternal love is one of his main values. He dreams of being a great writer, but feels he has missed his chance and survives thanks to his job as a teacher in a private school, presided over by Mr Deasy.

Physically, we know that he is puny and short-sighted. On the other hand, he has a talent for music and an excellent voice – a talent that Joyce himself also had. Stephen always behaves inappropriately towards other people: he does not like groups, does not manage to integrate into the various environments in which he develops and does not accept any part of his upbringing. He is always plagued by indecision, desire and regret, he has no confidence in himself, he puts himself down and he suffers from loneliness. He is also a calm, well-educated person who is good at debating and has an acute sense of compassion – particularly with his less talented students. Unlike Bloom, he does not have a particularly strong sex drive, although he does think about female nudity. He prefers to be surrounded by strong male characters, such as Buck Mulligan.

Although at the beginning of the story, Stephen seems like a suspicious, arrogant, abrupt character, only paying attention to ideas and seeking excellence in every domain, he becomes more and more human following his failure in Paris and particularly thanks to meeting Bloom. Next to him, he understands that intellect is nothing if you do not share it and that the meaning of life lies in your relationships with other people. Leopold allows him to get rid of his oversized ego and return to a simple life.

His name alludes to the architect in the myth of the Minotaur. Daedalus designed the labyrinth under the orders of Minos, intending to trap the monster inside. In *Ulysses*, Stephen Dedalus feels like the prisoner of another labyrinth: that of Dublin, which he hates due to its people who are stagnant, drunk and incapable of freeing themselves from English domination.

The first three chapters, 'The Telemachiad', focus on this protagonist. Stephen represents escape, from the town as much as from his own stagnation and uncertainty. He plays the role of Telemachus, Ulysses' son in Homer's version: younger than Leopold Bloom (Ulysses), he sees him as a father figure, compensating for the absence of his biological father. The tower in which he lives represents Ithaca, and his two rivals, Buck and Haines, symbolise Penelope's suitors. Just as it takes Ulysses time to regain his kingdom and find his son, the reader has to wait through several chapters before Stephen and Leopold meet and embark upon a true relationship in the drunken alleys of Dublin.

LEOPOLD BLOOM (ULYSSES)

The character Leopold Bloom appears in the second part of the novel, 'The Odyssey', and is the modern incarnation of Ulysses. Born in 1866, he is the only child of Ellen Higgins, an Irish Protestant, and Rudolph Virag, a Jew of Hungarian origin who converted to Protestantism. He is neurasthenic (suffers from mental and physical fragility), and his father ended up killing himself with poison. After his father's death, Leopold decides to convert to Catholicism so that he can marry Marion Tweedy (Molly) in 1888, a singer who is constantly touring all around Ireland and accumulates lovers – including the handsome singer Boylan. Two children were born of Molly and Leopold's marriage: Millicent (1889), nicknamed Milly, who is 15 and works for a photographer, and Rudy (1893), who lived for only 11 days. To meet his family's needs, Leopold works as an advertising agent for the *Evening Telegraph*.

Bloom is described as a simple, middle-class man with a discreet nature (when he is not under the influence of alcohol). He is benevolent, tolerant and very much in love with his wife, with whom, however, he no longer has sexual relations. This situation leads him to feel many urges throughout the novel, without ever managing the act – other than on his own.

His character seems almost a Christ-like figure due to his many acts of kindness: he helps a friend – without meaning to – to win a considerable amount of money at the horse racing, comes to the aid of a blind man, feeds animals, visits the sick, attends a funeral, etc. Paradoxically, he also takes on a comical side due to his clumsiness, his crazy ideas (checking, for example, if ancient statues have orifices), his mistakes during the Catholic rite, etc. There is also his attachment to excrement: many passages end in his farting, urinating or thinking about the sound of Molly on the chamber pot.

MALACHI MULLIGAN, KNOWN AS 'BUCK' (ANTINOUS)

Malachi Mulligan, a medical student, shares Stephen Dedalus' bedroom in Martello tower. This majestic, if plump, character has a deeply cynical personality and describes himself as a free-thinker, which allows him to blaspheme continually. He also enjoys slipping various quotes from poems into his speech, such as those of Algernon Swinburne (English poet, 1837-1909) and Walt Whitman (American poet, 1819-1892), or extracts from popular songs. He is rather jovial, light-hearted and does not have many worries; and as an extrovert is the complete opposite of Stephen's closed character. He is passionate about antiquity and about the philosophy of Nietzsche (German philosopher, 1844-1900), and his dream is to Hellenise Ireland (bring its culture closer to that of Ancient Greece). The permanent display of this culture shows Buck's pride, which reminds us of the same trait seen in Penelope's main suitor, Antinous.

Mulligan, who represents a form of bestiality, is, however, liked by all the other characters in the novel, apart from Stephen. The latter, although he lives with Mulligan and sees him every day, believes that he is a brute and condemns his behaviour and his beliefs. Nonetheless, Mulligan has already saved several people from drowning and treats Stephen generously, offering him clothes.

Joyce, when he created Buck, was inspired by one of his peers with whom he had shared a dormitory at Clongowes Wood College boarding school: Oliver Sint-John Gogarty (1878-1957), who was also a novelist and poet. The two boys often fought, much like Stephen and Buck, and Gogarty, moreover, did not hold back in criticising *Ulysses* after it was published.

MARION TWEEDY (PENELOPE)

Better known by her nickname Molly, Marion Tweedy is Leopold Bloom's wife. She represents Penelope. Molly, however, does not behave like the loving wife, patiently awaiting the return of her husband. Here their roles are reversed: when Leopold wanders the streets of Dublin, it is because he is waiting for his wife to come back to him.

Molly is a well-known singer and constantly on tour with others from the profession; she turns out to be unfaithful to her husband and prefers a certain Blazes Boylan, a singer described as an Adonis.

Molly's character has remained famous on account of the 18th episode of the novel: the monologue, void of punctuation, which she recites in a sort of sigh, close to an orgasm, and on which the story concludes. She is presented as much more sensual and physically desirable than both Leopold and Stephen, who move more in the intellectual sphere. During the monologue, Molly eventually accepts Leopold into her bed – just as Ulysses, on being reunited with Penelope, was restored to his dear Ithaca – and describes the moment they met in a story broken up periodically by the word 'yes', alluding to the pleasure she feels at being reunited with her husband.

When creating this character, Joyce was inspired by his wife, Nora Barnacle. Furthermore, the date of the beginning of the story, 16 June 1904, coincides with the writer's first date with his wife.

THE MAN IN THE MACINTOSH

This unnamed character only appears twice in the novel: first during the burial and secondly under the guise of Leopold Bloom's grandfather. No one has ever seen this person before and they are all unaware of the reason for his presence. When Bloom notices him, he finds that he looks like a devil.

Some critics believe that, in Ulysses, we could, in a way, see Leopold Bloom as Jesus, Stephen as the Holy Spirit, and the man in the macintosh as God himself. His long coat, which covers his whole body, only shows the face of God. His first appearance at the cemetery seems logical, as he would have come to find the soul of the deceased. Bloom, wondering who this "M'Intosh" is, thus asks the question of all of humanity: 'Who is God?'

His coat that hides him and his unexpected and nondescript appearances hark back to God's withdrawal from his Creation: he is both present and absent. As Leopold Bloom wanders from bar to bar and ends up in Bella Cohen's brothel, Lipoti Virag, his grandfather, appears to him as a ghost and is wearing the same macintosh: although it is not the same man from the cemetery, he is once again personifying God himself. We see another macintosh on a character from the 19 sketches of everyday life, Cashel Boyle O'Connor Fitzmaurice Tisdall Farrell. Once again, it is not the same man, but the fact that this coat comes back on different characters shows God's omnipresence; he is dispersed among the multitude.

ANALYSIS

Joyce, through Bloom's roaming, gives Ireland a mythical character. Daily life contains a sort of mythology that everyone can perceive. Behind every object and every meeting, there is a hidden meaning. Mortals can only try to decrypt what surrounds them, to know themselves and to understand the world. The roaming around Dublin represents that of every man trying to find himself in society.

Each episode corresponds to a new entry of the mythical, the organic and the religious or spiritual into daily life.

ALLUSIONS TO HOMER'S ODYSSEY

Firstly, the title of *Ulysses* establishes a direct link between the Homeric epic and Joyce's work. While in Homer's story, the journey is central, in Joyce's story, roaming has an intrinsic virtue and is linked to searching for a father figure. Stephen (Telemachus) is looking for a true father figure, beyond that of his biological father – let us not forget that this character is also the literary double of Joyce, who was not on good terms with his own alcoholic father, who was barely concerned with his family. The structure of the novel also recalls the tripartite structure of Homer's *Odyssey*.

Part one: 'The Telemachiad'

In the Greek story, this part is dedicated to the figure of Telemachus. The story begins when his father, Odysseus, has been missing for 20 years, and his mother, Penelope, is growing tired of rejecting marriage proposals from the numerous suitors who have moved into the palace. At the advice of the goddess Athena, Telemachus leaves Ithaca to go looking for Odysseus. During this trek, he meets King Nestor, then goes to Menelaus in Sparta.

While the Telemachiad contains four verses in Homer's version, it is made up of three episodes in Joyce's version:

- From the beginning of the novel, Buck Mulligan and Haines are portrayed in a negative light and are a direct reference to two of Penelope's suitors. Buck represents the violent, proud and brutal Antinous while Haines represents Eurymachus, who turns out to be a flirt and a manipulator. The way in which the former defends Stephen's recently deceased mother also seems suspect, as it is hardly in line with his usual thoughts. The latter also seems dubious, but this time regarding his mother-land: indeed, what Irishman would not despise an English invader who incessantly glorifies the history, folklore and society of Ireland while England is doing all it can to forbid them? The milk brought by the old woman signals his imminent departure; she symbolises Athena who urges Telemachus to embark on his journey.
- When he leaves the tower, Stephen (Telemachus) has a meeting with Mr Deasy who is Nestor's double.
- Then, when Stephen loses himself in thought on Sandymount beach, he imagines himself arguing with his uncle, Richie Goulding, a reference to Menelaus, about his situation and that of the world.

Part two: 'The Odyssey'

From the fourth episode onwards, Leopold Bloom's life is at the foreground and we therefore enter into Odysseus' journey. This part corresponds to ten years of roaming on the part of the Greek hero from the city of Troy to his homeland, Ithaca. In Homer's work, the story of these adventures takes up 16 verses, while in Joyce's work it is made up of 12 episodes.

- A comparison is made between Molly, the unfaithful wife, and the painting of a nymph hanging above the Bloom couple's bed. This comparison recalls Calypso, the nymph who was in love with Odysseus. In the same way as she imprisons Odysseus in the aim of marrying him, Molly traps Bloom in his own wishes and desires, constantly leaving him alone in Dublin.
- When Leopold goes to mass, he is surrounded by people who forget their worries and their rebellion against their own existence when they take communion and consume the host – just like the power of the lotus flowers on Odysseus' companions.
- The burial scene is linked to the divine capabilities of Tiresias. In the *Odyssey*, this character can summon dead people. He thus allows Odysseus to talk to the residents of hell. As for Joyce, the presence of the man in the macintosh is linked with life beyond death.
- The visit to the local paper directly refers to the episode with Aeolus, the wind keeper, who gives Odysseus a goatskin bag of wind to take him safely back to Ithaca. The hero's companions, convinced that the bag contains treasure, tear it open. Aeolus, furious, refuses to help

them twice. In Joyce's work, the keeper is represented by Myles Crawford, the head of the newspaper who, while at first pleasant towards Bloom, suddenly turns on him without any obvious reason, much like a crosswind.

- The Burton restaurant represents the dwelling of the Laestrygonians. Homer's cannibalistic giants feature among the establishment's clients who disgust Bloom with their enormous mouths that are incessantly chomping on and crushing various foods.

- The thesis on Shakespeare, defended by Stephen at the national library and listened to by a distracted Bloom, recalls the episode of Charybdis and Scylla, two sea monsters. Stephen thus explains that the English writer had two sides to him: on one hand, he portrayed himself in a favourable light and seemed to be a pleasant gentleman when he was in London; on the other hand, he could never be truly happy, as he was still devastated by his family disasters.

- The Sirens are present in the form of the waitresses with sharp tongues in the Ormond hotel restaurant. The Citizen, narrow-minded, nationalistic, slow-witted and ill-at-ease, represents the Cyclops Polyphemus whom Odysseus blinds.

- The erotic episode between Bloom and Gerty MacDowell recalls Odysseus' being saved by Nausicaa after he is shipwrecked.

- Bella Cohen, the brothel owner, is none other than the sorceress Circe. When they meet her and the other prostitutes, Leopold and Stephen develop lewd ideas, which recalls Odysseus' companions' being turned into pigs. Furthermore, the different voices and extracts of music they hear engulf the men, who lose touch with reality and are gripped by horrifying hallucinations.

Part three: 'The Nostos'

Finally, the three last episodes of the novel recall Odysseus' eventual return to Ithaca.

- The first part involves the reunion of Odysseus and Telemachus, who has not yet recognised his father, as he is disguised as Eumaeus, his swineherd. In Joyce's version, Bloom, who does not want to leave Stephen alone and lost, takes him under his wing and leads him to the cabman's shelter, owned by James Fitzharris, who represents Eumaeus.
- Bloom, once he is back home, thinks about Molly's lovers. This, however, does not stop him from loving his wife and remaining by her side. In the same way that Odysseus decides to empty his palace of all of Penelope's suitors, Bloom thus mentally uses the same tactic by putting aside the list of his wife's conquests.
- Finally, Molly's monologue closes the epic: just like Penelope, she leaves her lovers aside in favour of her husband, Leopold. She refuses to follow the same monotonous and disrespectful story towards the poor man, and says 'yes' to life. This speech can also be linked to Athena's defending Odysseus to his people who do not understand why he has killed so many people (Penelope's vile suitors).

A GENERIC AND ORGANIC COLLECTION

Joyce is in a constant literary search: he wants to innovate at all costs. *Ulysses* is a way for him to show that, as the situation in Dublin – which he criticises in his first novel, *Dubliners* (1914) – does not allow for innovation from the point of view of content, he must look for novelty elsewhere. Thus, there is no overarching feature of this novel, but a polymorphic *tour de force* of writing: each episode is created in the style of a particular genre. The reader therefore moves from the 'peristaltic' technique to monologue, dialectics or even something else.

GOOD TO KNOW

The adjective 'peristaltic' primarily means the progression of food during digestion, of its ingestion until it arrives at the rectum. To be completely digested, food moves with the help of muscle contractions. Reflecting this process, Joyce has an organic writing style that goes from contraction to relaxation.

Thus, in the episode that takes place primarily in Davy Byrne's bar at 1pm, the movements, thoughts and words of Leopold Bloom mimic the behaviour of his oesophagus: he walks, is hungry, is drawn to the smells of kitchen and, passing girls, is also animated by erotic impulses that titillate his senses. The contractions of his stomach grow as he has not been able to satisfy his appetite or drink a glass of wine. Once he has done this and is satisfied, he leaves to urinate and goes to satisfy

Its source of experimentation is therefore the genre. Joyce gave himself the objective of publishing a shapeshifting work which is called a novel and has the allure of a novel, but whose different sections are constructed with a narrative structure that is so varied that the work cannot be described as a novel in its entirety. Thus, in his stylistic search, Joyce emphasises parody, by taking the Homeric epic and placing it in a context of taverns and other vulgarities. He thus uses several narrative processes:

- Classic narrative, notably present in the first three episodes linked to Stephen ("Stately, plump Buck Mulligan came from the stairhead, bearing a bowl of lather on which a mirror and a razor lay crossed", p. 9);
- The theatrical replies accompanied by stage directions. We find them, for example, in the episode dedicated to the hallucinations of Bloom and Stephen in the streets of Dublin:

> "FLORRY: Sing us something. Love's old sweet song.
> STEPHEN: No voice. I am a most finished artist.
> Lynch, did I show you the letter about the lute?
> FLORRY: (SMIRKING) The bird that can sing and won't sing."
> (p. 761)

- The poetry in prose, as illustrated by Molly's monologue ("O that awful deepdown torrent O and the sea the sea crimson sometimes like fire", p. 1156);

- The journalistic writing, which is almost like a news item, of the 19 sketches;
- Etc.

Nothing is uniform and every episode has its own genre and style.

These stylistic changes follow the desire to focus on a particular organ of the human body. Although 'The Telemachiad' does not have one (as Stephen is still looking for sensory experiences), the following episodes are all linked to a different organ:

- The masturbation scene in the toilets and the direct showing of genitalia.
- Gerty showing what's under her skirt to Bloom, which signals the domination of eyes and sight. Most of Leopold's arousals come from this sense.
- The gathering in the newspaper's offices who sigh, exhale and spit out kernels, activities relating to the lungs.
- The absolute rationalisation of Shakespeare's texts displayed by Stephen uses the brain's precious intellect.
- Ears and hearing are used in the musical scenes at the Ormond hotel.
- The sketches in the fourth part, building to a climax, develop Mrs Purefoy's stages of childbirth and therefore refer to the uterus.
- Etc.

INTERTEXTUALITY

This diversity of writing, covering all genres and all organs and citing many authors, such as John Milton (English poet, 1608-1674), Charles Dickens (English novelist, 1812-1870) or Laurence Sterne (Irish novelist, 1713 -1768), also shows a relationship between the writings of the almost blind Joyce and the visually-impaired Jorge Luis Borges (1899-1986). Based on his readings of Joyce, among others, and a common narrative technique, the Argentine author advocates an unlimited practice of citation. And indeed, by taking the name of the of Greek antiquity, made famous due to the Homeric narrative, Joyce plunges immediately into this unlimited citation, that of a myth, that of the characters who populated his imagination and common cultural heritage, which, he says, has its roots in antiquity.

But the Irishman goes far beyond the theories developed by Borges a few decades later. While in the latter's work, citations are clearly indicated, notably by the presence of quotation marks, Joyce integrates them completely into his text, without any punctuation marks that would indicate a borrowing from another author. He wants indeed that through the process of intertextuality, his story tends towards the same universality as that presented by myths, that of any constituent story of human culture. His text was created by a writer - James Joyce - but, through the references made to other major components of literary and cultural heritage shared by humanity, he wants to be universal.

The author of *Ulysses* thus draws inspiration from his cultural baggage, his own internal 'library', which brings together all his readings of articles, essays and various novels. From these references, Joyce creates a text that has a broader form, compared with old literary knowledge. He picks, consciously or not, features of characters invented by other writers and is inspired to produce something new by myths or from a sentence from a book he read.

EPIPHANIES

Joyce, through a particular stylistic process that he himself conceived, reveals to his readers that a seemingly insignificant fact can reveal an episode that is spiritual or specific to a character. He calls this narrative technique 'epiphany'.

- In Roman antiquity, it marks the end of a winter solstice cycle. It is the longest night of the year and represents the triumph of light over dark.
- In Christianity, the Epiphany is a feast commemorating the birth of Christ and the visitation of the three wise men. This revelation of the coming of the Messiah marks the end of a spiritually sombre season, replaced by a period that is illuminated by the Divine Word.
- By extension, the word can refer to a stunning revelation of the depth of something.

To show the hidden meanings of daily life, he often uses ellipses. The hesitation and nonchalant nature of the text tell the reader that something else is going on behind the insignificant appearance of the words.

Just as the very nature of Jesus is revealed only to some, the objects and the world only reveal their true meaning in small traces that we must discern. If Joyce's epiphanies are not religious events, they are from the same concept of revelation: they illuminate daily life in its constant loss of meaning.

This sensitivity appears in dialogues without much consequence on the action: "One of the characteristics of epiphanies is that they are made up of completely banal, often interrupted, phrases. These broken phrases do not have a full meaning and thus produce a nonsense effect"[1] (Cassini, 2010). Epiphanies can also occur in the language, attitudes

1. This quotation has been translated by BrightSummaries.com

or actions of the characters, without them realising it. The hidden meaning is then perceived only by the reader.

This revelation, sometimes perceived by the Joycean character, sometimes only felt by the reader, is not far from the phenomena of manifestation, such as Proust's famous madeleine in *Swann's Way* (1913) or irregularity of some paving stones in *The Past Recaptured* (1927), which plunges the narrator into his memories. He suddenly detaches himself from reality to soak up the power of objects and have access to other meanings that he would not have seen otherwise.

While Joyce's epiphanies were created and are primarily developed in *A Portrait of the Artist as a Young Man* and *Dubliners*, they are found in *Ulysses* through scatological links that could pass for pure rudeness or for mundane details: consider, for example, the noise of Molly's urine falling into her chamberpot echoing the music heard in the hotel. Bloom's loud farts when coming out of a tavern imply for their part a link between natural elements and people throughout the narrative. Epiphanies in this novel are presented through the sounds emitted by characters. For Joyce, who became increasingly blind, it is not the things that we see that count, but the sounds that surround us - regardless of their nature.

This new concept of writing is conceived even more as the author, throughout his life, perceives the world in the manner of Claude Monet (French painter, 1840-1926) and his water lilies, with increasingly rare beams of light, while his eye condition worsens. Admittedly, this system of revelation through emotions that are specific to the subject, which considers a particular object, is not practiced only by Joyce, but he was the creator of the concept.

FURTHER REFLECTION

SOME QUESTIONS TO THINK ABOUT...

- Compare Homer's characters, Odysseus and Telemachus, to the characters of Leopold Bloom and Stephen Dedalus. What are their main similarities and differences? Use examples from the text.
- Describe the evolution of Stephen Dedalus in *Ulysses*, considering also extracts from *A Portrait of the Artist as a Young Man*.
- Give examples of other adaptations of the myth of Ulysses. How do the other works deal with this topic?
- How can banality be enhanced? Support your answer with examples from the text.
- Some critics claim that the episodes of this novel can be compared to the different parts of a mass. Give examples that support this theory.
- Describe the different narrative techniques used by Joyce in the different chapters of his work. Do they affect the meaning of the text?
- Which elements of the text show that Joyce was strongly against British domination over Ireland?
- Describe the similarities between *Ulysses* and Joyce's life.
- What links can we establish between this book and Dante's (Italian writer, 1265-1321) *Divine Comedy*?
- What role does Stephen Dedalus' thesis on *Hamlet* play in this novel?

We want to hear from you!
Leave a comment on your online library
and share your favourite books on social media!

FURTHER READING

REFERENCE EDITION

- Joyce, J. (2000) *Ulysses*. London: Penguin.

REFERENCE STUDIES

- Cassini, D. (2010) The James Joyce Experience. *Oxymoron*. [Online]. Issue 0. [Accessed 14 August 2015]. Available from: <http://revel.unice.fr/oxymoron/index.html?id=3070>
- De Souza, E. M. (1998) La poétique de la cécité chez Borges. *Variaciones Borges*. Issue 6.
- Joyce, J. (2000) *Finnegans Wake*. London: Penguin Classics.
- Joyce, J. (2000) *Dubliners*. London: Penguin Classics.
- Sobreira, R. (2013) Et soudain tout est devenu clair pour lui. La prise de conscience exprimée par l'épiphanie littéraire. *Revista Tabuleiro de Letras*. Issue 7.
- Tuduri, C. (2008) Une lecture de James Joyce. L'écriture, l'exil, l'alliance. *Études*. Vol. 409, p. 514.

Bright ≡Summaries.com

More guides to rediscover your love of literature

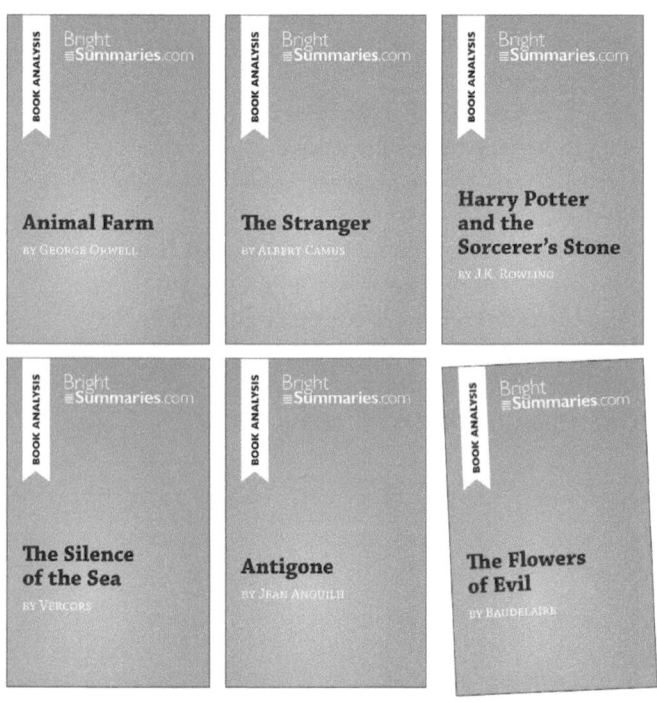

www.brightsummaries.com

www.brightsummaries.com

Ebook EAN: 9782806279637

Paperback EAN: 9782806284181

Legal Deposit: D/2016/12603/364

Cover: © Primento

Digital conception by Primento, the digital partner of publishers.